Valentine's Day

Valentine's Day

by Joyce K. Kessel
pictures by Karen Ritz

Carolrhoda Books
Minneapolis, Minnesota

Manufactured in the United States of America

This book is available in two editions:
Library binding by Carolrhoda Books, Inc.
Soft cover by First Avenue Editions
241 First Avenue North
Minneapolis, Minnesota 55401

LIBRARY OF CONGRESS CATALOGING IN PUBLICATION DATA

Kessel, Joyce.
　Valentine's Day.

　(Carolrhoda on my own books)
　SUMMARY: Explains the origins of Valentine's Day and describes the
traditions with which this special day is celebrated.
　1. St. Valentine's Day — Juvenile literature. [1. Valentine's Day]
I. Lund, Karen Ritz. II. Title.
GT4925.K47　　　　　　　　394.2'683　　　　　　　　81-3842
ISBN 0-87614-166-1 (lib. bdg.)　　　　　　　　　　　　AACR2
ISBN 0-87614-502-0 (pbk.)
　　　　4　5　6　7　8　9　10　98　97　96　95　94　93　92　91　90　89　88

to Kristie and Bradon

Bob's FLOWER SHOP

Every year, on February 14,

we celebrate Valentine's Day.

People send cards to their friends.

They give presents to their sweethearts.

Flower stores sell more flowers

than on almost any other day of the year.

Valentine's Day is a popular holiday.

And it has had a long history.

It began over 2,700 years ago.

But it was very different then

from what it is today.

7

Valentine's Day began in Rome.

Rome is a city in Italy.

When Rome was built,

over 2,700 years ago,

hungry wolves lived all around it.

At night they howled at the city gates.

They killed the sheep outside the walls.

Sometimes they even killed people.

The Romans were afraid of the wolves.

So they prayed to Lupercus.

Lupercus was the Roman god
who watched over sheep and shepherds.
The Romans held a holiday for him
each year.
They asked him to keep them safe.
They asked him to drive the wolves away.
Finally the wolves did disappear.
But by then the Romans
were used to Lupercus's holiday.
They enjoyed it.
So they kept on celebrating it.

But as the years passed,

the holiday changed.

Lupercus was not

as important to the Romans

as he used to be.

Slowly his holiday became

a holiday for Juno instead.

Juno was the queen of the Roman gods.

She ruled over marriage.

The holiday for Juno was different

from the holiday for Lupercus.

It was a holiday of love.

During Juno's holiday,
Roman girls wrote their names
on pieces of paper.

They dropped the papers into a jar.
Then Roman boys drew them out.
The girl whose name a boy drew
became his partner for the holiday.

By the year 496, the Christian church
had become powerful.

Pope Gelasius was head of the church.

He didn't believe in the old Roman gods.

He didn't want people to worship them.

He didn't like Juno's holiday at all.

So he tried to stop it.

But he could not.

People enjoyed it too much.

So Pope Gelasius decided to make
the old holiday into a church holiday.

First he needed a reason for a holiday.

He looked around for a saint to honor.

And he found one named Valentine.

Valentine died on February 14, 269.

Juno's holiday was on February 15.

Pope Gelasius ended Juno's holiday.

He changed it to Saint Valentine's Day.

Saint Valentine

Pope Gelasius knew

which Saint Valentine he chose.

But today no one is sure.

In those days there were

at least three saints named Valentine.

Some books say there were eight!

But two are talked about most.

Both were priests.

Both were killed by Emperor Claudius.

He was called "Claudius the Cruel."

Claudius was angry because

no one would go to war.

The men wanted to stay in Rome.

They didn't want to leave their wives.

So Claudius said no one else

could get married!

Valentine felt sorry for the people

who were in love.

He married them secretly.

But Claudius found out.

"Throw that man into jail!" he said.

Later Claudius had Valentine killed.

There is a second story
about another Valentine.
Claudius put this Valentine in jail too.

Claudius didn't like Christians.

Valentine had helped many Christians.

While Valentine was in jail,

he met the jailer's daughter.

She was blind.

Valentine performed a miracle.

He made the girl see.

This made Claudius angry.

So he killed this Valentine too.

But before Valentine died,

he sent a poem to the little girl.

He signed it, "from your Valentine."

No one knows if these stories
really happened.
But whoever Saint Valentine was,
February 14 became his holiday.
As time went on,
the Christian church spread.
Because Valentine's Day
was now a church holiday,
it spread too.
By the year 1400,
people in countries all over Europe
celebrated Valentine's Day.
Pope Gelasius had planned
Valentine's Day
as a religious holiday.

But in most countries

it didn't work out that way.

People enjoyed the old holiday of love

too much to change it.

In Sicily, girls got up early
on Valentine's Day.
Each girl stood at her window.
She wanted to be sure to see
the first man who passed by.

He, or a man who looked like him,
was supposed to marry her.
If no man passed by,
it meant that the girl
would not marry that year.

In Denmark, men sent white flowers,
called snowdrops,
to their sweethearts.
Danish people thought
snowdrops brought good luck.

But in Scotland, people thought
snowdrops brought bad luck.
If a man gave snowdrops to a woman,
she would not marry that year.

In England, people were very friendly
on Valentine's morning.
"Good morning," they called out
to their families and friends.

"It's Valentine's Day."
Whoever said this first
got a present from the other person.

When the English came to America,

they brought Valentine's Day with them.

But it didn't become popular right away.

Life in the New World

was very hard at first.

People had no time for Valentine's Day.

But as life got easier,

Valentine's Day caught on.

Now over 150,000,000 valentines are sent

in the U.S. and Canada every year!

Who sent the first valentine?

One legend says it was Saint Valentine.

He could pick violets

through his jail window.

He wrote messages on the leaves.

Then birds delivered the messages.

Another legend tells us
that the first valentine
was made in the year 1415.
England and France were at war, and
Charles, Duke of Orleans, was captured.
The English locked him
in the Tower of London.
Charles missed his wife very much.
So he sent her love poems.

These stories are just legends though.

No one knows who really made

the first valentine.

But by the year 1600,

many people were sending them.

Some people copied poems.

Some made up their own.

Then they decorated their cards.

Since the 1800s,

valentines have been made by machines.

♥ ♥

LOVE OFFICE TELEGRAM

Charges to pay....
half as much again

If the receiver of a loveland message doubts
he or she may have it repeated verbally on paying a
the sender. In the event of a mutual confession b
the amount of happiness will be great.

Office of origin ___THE NEART___ handed to a ___SWE___
by a ___LOVE L___

When shall we two meet again?
In thunder, lightening, or in rain
In wet weather, or in shine?
Or on the feast of Valentine

When the tone of the reply to this telegr__ is de
number of words fall short of what might b__ __ the
reply must pay for any excess of cruel__ __ brea
confiding heart.

Five kisses per word

JUST A LITTLE VALENTINE!

Some have been plain.

Some have been fancy.

Some have been funny.

Some have been sweet.

Some have even been mean.

A VALENTINE SOUVENIR

POPPING THE QUESTION
Yes, pop some corn for me, my swee
Tis good for the digestion:
And while you pop the corn, my de
Why, I'll just pop—
the question

Two Spoon

Valentines have changed over the years, just like clothes.

In the 1830s,
valentines were very fancy.
Some were made of silver.
Others were made of shells or lace.
They cost as much as $10!

In the 1860s and 1870s,

valentines got mean.

They made fun of fat people.

They made fun of thin people.

They made fun of almost everyone.

These cards made many people unhappy.

They were called "penny dreadfuls."

It was a good name for them!

They cost a penny.

And they were dreadful!

Because of them, Valentine's Day

was less popular for a while.

39

Around 1910, valentines became nice again.

The decorations were simple.

And the poems were friendly.

This is how most valentines are today.

To

To my Valentine

We see the same pictures used
again and again on valentines.
Red hearts are used most often.
They have stood for love
since ancient times.

Ribbons go back to the days
when ladies gave ribbons
to their favorite knights.
The knights carried those ribbons
when they went to war.

Souvenir of St Valentine's Day

Roses too are often seen on valentines.

The rose is called the flower of love.

Violets also stand for love.

This probably goes back

to the story of Saint Valentine.

43

We often see lace on valentines.

The word "lace" comes from a Latin word.

Latin was the language
that the Romans spoke.

The Latin word means "to catch."

Lace was supposed to catch
the heart of a loved one.

The chubby boy with wings
who we see on many valentines
is Cupid.

Cupid was the Roman god of love.
He always carries a bow and arrows.
He uses them to shoot love
into people's hearts.

This year, people in England,
France, the United States, and Canada
will be sending valentines.
In England and France,
people send valentines
only to sweethearts.
They do not usually sign the cards.
The person who gets the card
may never know who sent it!

But in the U.S. and Canada,
we enjoy sending valentines
to our families and friends too.
Valentine's Day has become a day
when we remember to tell our friends
that we like them.

About the Author

Joyce K. Kessel's previous ON MY OWN book, HALLOWEEN, was a 1981 Children's Choice. Ms. Kessel was born and grew up in North Dakota, and for eleven years worked as a speech therapist and school administrator in Puerto Rico. She now lives in Minneapolis.

About the Artist

Karen Ritz is no stranger to ON MY OWN books either. Her illustrations for CORNSTALKS AND CANNONBALLS by Barbara Mitchell "catch characters on the spur of action" (—Language Arts) and "accurately depict historic details" (—Instructor). Ms. Ritz holds a degree in children's literature and illustration from the University of Minnesota.